When You Pray as a Small Group

WHEN YOU PRAY

as a Small Group

Rueben P. Job and Sally D. Sharpe

Abingdon Press
Nashville

WHEN YOU PRAY
AS A SMALL GROUP

Copyright © 2010 by Abingdon Press

ISBN 978-1-426-70900-5

10 11 12 13 14 15 16 17 18 19—10 9 8 7 6 5 4 3 2 1
MANUFACTURED IN THE UNITED STATES OF AMERICA

CONTENTS

INTRODUCTION

There are many ways to grow and mature as a Christian, but perhaps none is more important than developing a pattern of prayer that leads to a closer walk with God. Cultivating a meaningful prayer life is something we are to do not only in private but also in community—both when we are alone and when we meet together. In fact, one of the most effective ways we may begin, renew, or deepen our prayer life is to pray regularly with a group of faithful followers of Jesus Christ.

This guide is intended to assist small groups in the exploration and practice of prayer. It may be used by prayer groups, Sunday school classes, Bible study groups, committees/teams, or any small group desiring to grow closer to God and to one another through prayer. Designed to be used in conjunction with the resource *When You Pray: Daily Practices for Prayerful Living* by Rueben P. Job (Abingdon Press, 2009), this guide presents five session plan templates, offering choices for different types of groups with different needs and interests:

Discussion-based
Activity-based
Introspective
Arts-focused
Habit Breaker

Though the templates roughly follow the same basic outline—which is intentionally linked to the pattern of prayer outlined in *When You Pray* and based on the pattern of prayer taught and modeled by Jesus in the Gospels—each template has unique nuances, distinctions, and modifications designed specifically for a given group or approach. To use a template to create your own group session, simply select a weekly reading from *When You Pray* and "plug in" the appropriate Scriptures and other material as indicated in the template. The weekly readings in *When You Pray*, which are numbered from 1-56, begin with the first week of Advent and continue throughout the seasons of the church year. You may select material for your group sessions according to the season and corresponding common lectionary readings, or you may choose to select material according to topic or theme. Whether you need group sessions for one month, one quarter, or an entire year, you will find ample material in *When You Pray* from which to choose.

Each of the five templates included in this guide outlines a session plan of just under 60 minutes, with suggestions for decreasing or extending the session if desired. Following each template, you will find a list of "Prayerwork" suggestions (prayer activity ideas) suited for the specified kind of group. For example, discussion-based Prayerwork ideas are provided for discussion-based groups, action-oriented Prayerwork ideas are provided for activity-based groups, and so forth. Time has been allotted for one Prayerwork activity per group session. Choose from those provided in this guide, or find other prayer activities you would like to try by searching the Internet or your local library or bookstore.

As you follow this simple guide to create your own group sessions, feel free to choose one session template or to mix them up as you wish to meet the needs and preferences of your group. The purpose of this resource is not to encourage a legalistic or rote practice of prayer, but to offer guidance, encouragement, and practical help for cultivating a meaningful prayer experience suited to your particular group.

As you establish the habit and pattern of praying together as a group in the coming weeks, you are likely to find that your own personal practice of prayer is both enriched and strengthened. May you and those joining with you discover anew the life-giving power of prayer!

ORIENTATION SESSION

(Approximately 60 minutes)

Materials Needed:

Bible(s), copies of *When You Pray: Daily Practices for Prayerful Living* for all participants, any items needed for your Prayerwork activity

Opening (5 minutes)

Welcome participants and open with prayer. Read aloud a brief Scripture and offer a prayer in response. You may say your own prayer or use the following:

> Loving God, you are a God of relationship. You love us without limit and call us into relationship with you through your Son, Jesus Christ. You make your home within us, indwelling us with your Holy Spirit. You are our ever-present companion, our loving and wise guide, our very source of life and strength. We long to know you more—to draw nearer to you through prayer so that we may walk more closely with you each day and live faithfully and fully as followers of Jesus Christ. Guide us in this process. "Lord, teach us to pray."* We ask it in the name of Jesus. Amen.

*Luke 11:1

Introduction (5-10 minutes)

In advance, familiarize yourself with the introduction of this book. Present the information found there in your own words, noting that one of the most effective ways to cultivate a meaningful prayer life is to explore and practice prayer in community.

Announce that a variety of small groups will be forming in the coming weeks for that very purpose. (Indicate the number of weeks that groups will be meeting, or acknowledge that each group may make this decision.)

Explain that although the groups will use the same resource— *When You Pray: Daily Practices for Prayerful Living* by Rueben P. Job—they will have the option of choosing one or more styles or approaches designed to meet different needs and interests. Note that groups may choose one style or approach or mix them up from week to week as they choose.

Briefly present and explain the five group options to participants:

Discussion-based – for those who prefer to emphasize group discussion

Activity-based – for those desiring more hands-on activity

Introspective – for those who prefer reflective, self-examining practices such as meditation and journaling

Arts-focused – for those who enjoy various modes of artistic expression

Habit Breaker – for those eager to break out of old habits and try new approaches

Overview (15 minutes)

In advance, become familiar with each of the five group session templates. Note that 1) the session outline is basically the same from group to group (with the exception of the Introspective Group, which substitutes Journaling Time for Group Discussion/ Application), and 2) the distinctions or nuances among the groups are found in *how* each segment of the session outline is approached or carried out.

If possible, provide copies of *When You Pray* for all participants, or have participants share. Present the basic outline of the group session:

Opening
Invitational Prayer
Scripture Reading
Devotional Reading
Group Discussion/Application (or Journaling Time)
Prayerwork
Group Prayer
A Time of Commitment
Closing

As you move through each segment of the outline, explaining what will happen at that time, note any nuances or distinctions suggested for each of the five groups. For example, a candle and instrumental music are added to the Opening for introspective groups, while arts-focused groups are encouraged to use a visual element during this time. Likewise, the Group Prayer becomes more active for activity-based groups with the addition of doodling, drawing, or movement, while arts-focused groups are instructed to create a prayer mural. During the time ordinarily set aside for Group Discussion, introspective groups engage in journaling instead. And so forth.

Prayerwork (15-20 minutes)

Highlight the importance of the Prayerwork activities, noting that a list of suggestions is provided for each of the five groups. Groups are encouraged to select one idea for each session, and/or to create/find their own prayer activities tailored to address their specific needs and interests. (A multitude of ideas may be found by searching the Internet or a local library or bookstore.)

In advance, choose a Prayerwork activity and gather any necessary materials. Lead the group through the exercise at this time.

Questions (5 minutes)

Have a time for questions and answers. Write down any questions you are unable to answer at this time, and get back to the individual with an answer later.

Closing (5 minutes)

Invite participants to join you in the Closing from the sample session for discussion-based groups (found on page 64).

Read aloud the following Scripture blessing:

> The LORD bless you and keep you;
> the LORD make his face to shine
>   upon you, and be gracious to you;
> the LORD lift up his countenance upon you,
>   and give you peace. *(Numbers 6:24-26)*

Follow the blessing with a benediction that the group may recite together. For example, you might say together, "May the Lord bless you and keep you," "Live in peace, and the God of love and peace will be with you," "The grace of our Lord Jesus Christ be with you," or some other benediction of your choosing.

In advance, create five sign-up sheets—one for each of the five group styles—or one sign-up sheet with a column where individuals may note their preferred group style. Allow space for name, phone number, and email address. Invite those who are interested in joining/leading a group to sign up on their way out.

GROUP SESSION TEMPLATES

DISCUSSION-BASED GROUP
Session Plan Template

(Note: This template outlines a session of just under 60 minutes. To decrease the time, eliminate one or more segments of your choosing. To extend the session, allow more time for Prayerwork and/or Group Discussion/Application.)

Materials Needed:
Bible(s), *When You Pray: Daily Practices for Prayerful Living*, any items needed for your Prayerwork activity

Opening (1-3 minutes)
"Becoming Aware of God's Presence"

The opening is a time to prepare yourselves for encountering God. After welcoming participants, read aloud a brief Scripture passage intended to help group members focus their minds and hearts on recognizing and welcoming God's presence (see "Becoming Aware of God's Presence" in *When You Pray*).

Invitational Prayer (3 minutes)
"Inviting God's Intervention"

Spend a few moments inviting God to act—in your lives, your families, your small group, your church, your community, and your world. After reading aloud a brief Scripture or text (see "Inviting God's Intervention" in *When You Pray*), offer a prayer in response. Determine in advance who will pray aloud for the group each week.

Scripture Reading (3-5 minutes)

"Listening for God's Voice"

Open yourselves to what God is saying to you through the Scriptures. Read aloud one or two key Scripture readings from those provided for the week (see "Listening for God's Voice" in *When You Pray*). Select the reading(s) prior to the group session. If you like, have a different group member read the Scripture selection(s) each week.

(Note: In *When You Pray*, three choices are provided for the Sunday Scripture drawn from the common lectionary. If your congregation follows the Ecumenical Sunday Lectionary Scripture readings and you wish to choose a Sunday Scripture for your group session, a chart in the back of *When You Pray* will help you to identify which cycle to use—A, B, or C.)

Devotional Reading (5 minutes)

"Essay / Quotations"

Read aloud the brief essay written by Rueben P. Job provided for the week, as well any quotations that you would like to share (see "Essay" and "Quotations" in *When You Pray*).

Group Discussion/Application (10 minutes)

"Reflection Time"

Take time to reflect on what you have read and heard and consider how it applies to your lives. In advance of the session, choose from the following questions, or feel free to write your own.

- What is God saying to you through what we have shared today?

- How does today's theme apply to a particular situation or circumstance you are dealing with currently?
- What life experiences have enlightened your understanding of today's theme?
- What questions have been raised by today's readings?
- How is God calling you to respond—as individuals and as a group?

Prayerwork (15-20 minutes)

Choose one of the Prayerwork ideas for discussion-based groups found on pages 19–23, or create/find your own prayer activity.

Group Prayer (5 minutes)
"Making Our Requests Known"

Enter into a time of prayer in which group members are invited to pray silently and/or aloud in response to specific prayer prompts. Pause after reading each prompt. Use the following prompts, or feel free to create your own:

Almighty God, we offer now our praise and thanks for who you are, what you have done, and what you have revealed to us today…

Loving Creator, we now offer our prayers for our world and its people and leaders…

We lift up to you, O God, our church and its leaders…

Gracious God, receive now our prayers on behalf of those in our circle of care or concern…

Finally, Lord, we submit our personal needs and requests…

A Time of Commitment (2 minutes)
"Offering of Self to God"

Follow the group prayer with a time of commitment in which you offer your very lives to God—all that you have, all that you are, and all that you hope to become. Surrender control as you invite God to do what is best—confident that God will meet your needs and bless you as you give your life to the work of God in this world. Use the Scripture or text provided in the weekly reading (see "Offering of Self to God" in *When You Pray*), or offer your own prayer of commitment.

Closing (2 minutes)
"Blessing"

End the session with a blessing. Read aloud the blessing provided in the weekly reading (see "Blessing" in *When You Pray*), and follow it with a benediction that the group may recite together each week. For example, you might say together, "May the Lord bless you and keep you," "Live in peace, and the God of love and peace will be with you," "The grace of our Lord Jesus Christ be with you," or some other benediction of your choosing.

Prayerwork Ideas for Discussion-Based Groups

- Invite participants to define prayer. Ask: What is it? How do we do it? Why do we do it? Discuss what we can do to prevent our prayer time from becoming a "one-way conversation."

- Ask participants what they like most about prayer and what they find easiest. Then discuss what they find most difficult about prayer. Brainstorm ways you might address some of these difficulties.

- Take turns sharing and discussing your own prayer practices, routines, and rituals as well as helpful hints for establishing a regular prayer habit.

- Read aloud 1 Thessalonians 5:16-18. Discuss what it means to pray continually and how we can do this. Talk about how everyday activities can be constant reminders to pray. Give several examples to illustrate:

  - As you exercise, pray for the strength and ability to do God's will.
  - As you shower, pray for God's cleansing and forgiveness of your sins.
  - As you drive to work, pray for your boss and co-workers.
  - As you drive past a church, pray for that church, for your church, and for the church universal—as well as for Christian pastors and leaders.
  - As you watch the news, pray about the circumstances being reported.
  - As you find yourself worrying, turn your worries into prayers.

- As you make a purchase or balance your checkbook, say a prayer of thanksgiving for God's provision.

Have the group contribute to the list. Write their ideas on a board or chart.

- Have a prayer Q&A time when participants can take turns asking questions of the group. Do this once, or repeat the exercise at two or more sessions. Here are some sample questions participants might ask:

    - Where do you like to pray, and why?
    - When is your favorite time of day to pray, and why?
    - What helps you to enter into a time of prayer?
    - How do you keep your mind from wandering when you pray?
    - Do you structure your prayer time or follow any pattern? If so, how?
    - Do you use any books or other resources in your prayer time, and if so, what?
    - Have you ever had a prayer partner, and how did that work?
    - When and how do you pray with your family?
    - Have you had "dry" periods when you found it difficult to pray? If so, what did you do?
    - What hinders your prayer time/prayer life?
    - How has prayer enriched your life?

- Discuss various forms, methods, and models of prayer, such as breath prayer, guided prayer, arrow prayers, *lectio divina*, centering prayer, the ACTS prayer model (adoration, confession, thanksgiving, supplication), and so forth. Present and discuss a variety of prayer methods, or focus on one method each session. You might ask each participant to research a different method, and then have one person present his or her findings each week.

- Learn about the prayer methods of other religions. Ask a different member each session to bring a topic to present and discuss. Possibilities might include Islamic calls to prayer, uses of prayer beads and rosaries, or icons. (See the article by Marilyn Thornton on page 47 and the article on prayer beads by Sally Dyck on page 156 in *Becoming a Praying Congregation* [Abingdon, 2009].)

- Explore the phrases of the Lord's Prayer by having participants break into pairs or groups of three. Give each pair/group an index card with a phrase from the Lord's Prayer and questions about that phrase written on it (see below). Have the pairs/groups discuss the questions for about 5 minutes. Then reconvene and allow each pair/group to share their insights.

OUR FATHER IN HEAVEN
- What does this phrase tell us about God and God's character?
- How does viewing God as "Father" help or hinder your prayers? Why?
- Of what does the word "our" remind us? Why is this important for us to remember?
- What do the words "in heaven" tell us—about God, ourselves, our destiny?

HALLOWED BE YOUR NAME
- What does "hallowed" mean?
- Why is it important to acknowledge that God's name is holy?
- How should this affect or shape our prayers?

YOUR KINGDOM COME

- What is God's kingdom, and what does it mean to pray for it to "come"?
- How is God's kingdom both here now and yet to come?
- What can we do to extend the kingdom of God upon the earth now?
- What does the Bible tells us about the future kingdom of God?

YOUR WILL BE DONE ON EARTH AS IT IS IN HEAVEN

- What are we asking when we pray this part of the prayer?
- How can we know God's will?
- How can we participate in bringing God's will on earth?
- What does it mean to submit or surrender ourselves to God's will? Give an example of what this might "look like" in an individual's life.

GIVE US THIS DAY OUR DAILY BREAD

- What does this phrase mean? What are we asking God to do for us?
- Why is it important to acknowledge that God is our Provider?
- How does God use us to help care for others—to be God's hands on earth?

AND FORGIVE US OUR TRESPASSES/SINS

- Why is it important to ask for God's forgiveness?
- When, and for what, should we ask God's forgiveness?
- What can hinder us from asking for and receiving God's forgiveness?

AS WE FORGIVE THOSE WHO TRESPASS/SIN AGAINST US

- Why is it important to forgive others?
- What did Jesus say about the necessity of forgiving others?
- What happens when we forgive others?
- What hinders us from forgiving others?
- What can help us to overcome these hindrances?

AND LEAD US NOT INTO TEMPTATION

- What is temptation?
- Is it a sin to be tempted?
- In what ways is this phrase a prayer for protection?
- Why does God sometimes allow us to be tempted?
- What does God promise us when we are tempted?
- What can we do to avoid yielding to temptation?

BUT DELIVER US FROM EVIL

- What does "evil" refer to here?
- What does it mean to be "delivered" from evil?
- How can we live victoriously in a world full of evil?

ACTIVITY-BASED GROUP
Session Plan Template

(Note: This template outlines a session of just under 60 minutes. To decrease the time, eliminate one or more segments of your choosing. To extend the session, allow more time for Prayerwork and/or Group Discussion/Application.)

Materials Needed:
Bible(s), *When You Pray: Daily Practices for Prayerful Living*, large wipe-off board and dry erase markers (or butcher/bulletin board paper and colorful markers), plenty of paper and pencils for everyone, colored pencils or markers, any items needed for your Prayerwork activity

Opening (1-3 minutes)
"Becoming Aware of God's Presence"

The opening is a time to prepare yourselves for encountering God. After welcoming participants, invite participants to stand as you read aloud a brief Scripture passage intended to help them focus their minds and hearts on recognizing and welcoming God's presence (see "Becoming Aware of God's Presence" in *When You Pray*).

Invitational Prayer (3 minutes)
"Inviting God's Intervention"

Invite God to act in tangible ways during and following today's group session. First, read aloud the brief Scripture or text provided in the weekly reading (see "Inviting God's Intervention" in

When You Pray). Then invite group members to come to the board and write sentence prayers expressing specific ways they would like to see God act—in their lives, their families, your small group, your church, your community, and the world. (Another idea is to have participants write with colorful markers on butcher/bulletin board paper taped to the wall.)

Scripture Reading (3-5 minutes)
"Listening for God's Voice"

Open yourselves to what God is saying to you through the Scriptures. In advance of the session, choose one or two key Scripture readings from those provided for the selected week (see "Listening for God's Voice" in *When You Pray*). Read the passage(s) aloud by having a different group member read each verse. Instruct those who are not reading aloud to listen for and write down 1-3 key words that "jump out" or speak to them most strongly. Share the words aloud, without discussion, and/or write them on a board, chart, or poster for display throughout the session.

(Note: In *When You Pray*, three choices are provided for the Sunday Scripture drawn from the common lectionary. If your congregation follows the Ecumenical Sunday Lectionary Scripture readings and you wish to choose a Sunday Scripture for your group session, a chart in the back of *When You Pray* will help you to identify which cycle to use—A, B, or C.)

Devotional Reading (5 minutes)
"Essay / Quotations"

Read aloud the brief essay written by Rueben P. Job provided for the week, as well as any quotations that you would like to share (see "Essay" and "Quotations" in *When You Pray*). If you like, invite a different group member to read aloud each week.

Group Discussion/Application (5-10 minutes)
"Reflection Time"

Take a few minutes to briefly respond to what you have heard, seen, and experienced together, considering how it applies to your lives. In advance of the session, choose from the following questions, or feel free to write your own.

- What is God saying to you through what we have shared today?
- What questions have been raised by today's session?
- How is God calling you to respond—as individuals and as a group?

Prayerwork (15-20 minutes)

Choose one of the Prayerwork ideas for activity-based groups found on pages 30–31. (Note: The prayer activity should be the focal point of your group session.)

Group Prayer (5 minutes)
"Making Our Requests Known"

Invite group members to try an active method of prayer by drawing or doodling in response to prayer prompts that you read aloud (see next page). Explain that doodling invites our bodies into prayer and helps us to concentrate better. Give each participant a sheet of paper and one or more markers or colored pencils. Instruct them to quiet their minds and listen for what God might be saying to them as each prayer prompt is read. Participants are likely to find that the images and words they doodle on their papers will stick in their minds and come back to them long after the session is over.

OR

Invite group members to pray aloud or silently in response to the prayer prompts. Have participants stand and encourage them to allow their bodies to move as they pray (whether praying silently or aloud). Explain that some of us focus better when we move. Our bodies are no longer a distraction but a participant in prayer. Psalm 35:10 says, "My whole being will exclaim, / 'Who is like you, O LORD?' " (NIV). This is an opportunity to involve our whole beings in prayer.

Use the following prompts, or feel free to create your own. Pause for one full minute after reading each prompt:

> Almighty God, we offer now our praise and thanks for who you are, what you have done, and what you have revealed to us today...

> Loving Creator, we now offer our prayers for our world and its people and leaders...

> We lift up to you, O God, our church and its leaders...

> Gracious God, receive now our prayers on behalf of those in our circle of care or concern...

> Finally, Lord, we submit our personal needs and requests...

A Time of Commitment (2 minutes)
"Offering of Self to God"

Follow the group prayer with a time of commitment in which you offer your very lives to God—all that you have, all that you are, and all that you hope to become. Surrender control as you invite God to do what is best—confident that God will meet your needs and bless you as you give your life to the work of God in this world.

Read aloud the Scripture or text provided in the weekly reading (see "Offering of Self to God" in *When You Pray*), or offer your own prayer of commitment. As the prayer is offered, invite participants to assume a physical posture of prayer that symbolizes submission and dependence—kneeling, bowing, lying prostrate, extending hands upward, etc. After the prayer, ask each participant to write on a piece of paper a word, phrase, or sentence expressing a personal commitment to God. Have participants fold their papers and take them with them as a reminder in the coming week.

Closing (2 minutes)
"Blessing"

End the session with a blessing. Read aloud the blessing provided in the weekly reading (see "Blessing" in *When You Pray*), and follow it with a benediction activity that the group may repeat each week. For example, your group may choose to sing a benediction, such as "May the Lord Bless You and Keep You." Or you might say a verse or benediction together as you "sign" it using American Sign Language or motions you create. Or simply offer your own verbal blessings and expressions of love to one another as you are leaving. Choose an activity that fits the personality of your group.

Prayerwork Ideas for
Activity-Based Groups

- Start a prayer project as a group. Try something tangible such as creating an altar cloth, quilt, prayer beads, or other project and work on it periodically or at each session. Pray over each part/section that you make.

- Learn about the prayer methods of other religions. Ask a different member each session to bring a topic to present and discuss. Possibilities might include Islamic calls to prayer, uses of prayer beads and rosaries, or icons. (See the article by Marilyn Thornton on page 47 and the article on prayer beads by Sally Dyck on page 156 in *Becoming a Praying Congregation*.)

- Describe/discuss ways to encourage or facilitate the practice of prayer, such as setting up a prayer station, subscribing to a Twitter service, and so forth. (See the article by Ben Simpson on "Social Media and Spiritual Formation" on page 116 in *Becoming a Praying Congregation*.)

- Work together to write your own personal prayers using the Lord's Prayer as a model—1) address God, 2) give thanks, etc.

- Brainstorm how to start a "Prayer Line" in your congregation. Talk to your pastor or church leadership about the possibility. This can be done many ways (telephone, email, website, broadcast). Read an example of how one church opened a call line during its worship service, taking calls and praying with callers, and came to have a 24/7 call line for prayer messages (see page 102 in *Becoming a Praying Congregation*).

- Take a prayer walk through your church/church campus. Visit various stations or locations—such as the sanctuary, prayer room/chapel, various classrooms, baby nursery, fellowship hall, library, offices, etc.—and pray briefly in each one. Pray for the individuals who gather and the activities that take place in each location.

- Discuss how to "pray the Scriptures" and then practice it together. Choose 1-2 psalms or other familiar passages and work together to fashion them into personal prayers. Write the prayers on a board or chart. Then have each participant select a Scripture and write his or her own personalized prayer. Share as time allows.

- Plan a special prayer service that your group may host at a later date. Consider whether you will invite a particular group within your church, the entire congregation, and/or the community.

INTROSPECTIVE GROUP
Session Plan Template

(Note: This template outlines a session of just under 60 minutes. To decrease the time, eliminate one or more segments of your choosing. To extend the session, allow more time for Prayerwork and/or Journaling.)

Materials Needed:
Bible(s), *When You Pray: Daily Practices for Prayerful Living*, journals or notebooks (one for each participant), pens or pencils, candle and matches or lighter, instrumental music CD and CD player, any items needed for your Prayerwork activity

Opening (1-3 minutes)
   "Becoming Aware of God's Presence"

The opening is a time to relax and prepare yourselves for encountering God. Light a candle to acknowledge God's presence, and let the candle burn throughout the session. After welcoming participants, read aloud a brief Scripture passage intended to help group members focus their minds and hearts on recognizing and welcoming God's presence (see "Becoming Aware of God's Presence" in *When You Pray*). Then invite group members to sit quietly for a moment, meditating on the verses they heard as they relax and calm their bodies, minds, and spirits. You may want to play quiet instrumental music during this time.

Invitational Prayer (3 minutes)

"Inviting God's Intervention"

Spend a few moments inviting God to act—in your lives, your families, your small group, your church, your community, and your world. After reading aloud the brief Scripture or text provided in the weekly reading (see "Inviting God's Intervention" in *When You Pray*), offer a prayer in response. Determine in advance who will pray aloud for the group each week. You may choose to continue the music during this time.

Scripture Reading (3-5 minutes)

"Listening for God's Voice"

Open yourselves to what God is saying to you through the Scriptures. Read aloud one or two key Scripture readings from those provided for the week (see "Listening for God's Voice" in *When You Pray*). Select the reading(s) prior to the group session. (Note: You may want to choose a different reader each week.) Instruct participants to write meaningful words or phrases or make sketches in their journals as the Scripture is read.

(Note: In *When You Pray*, three choices are provided for the Sunday Scripture drawn from the common lectionary. If your congregation follows the Ecumenical Sunday Lectionary Scripture readings and you wish to choose a Sunday Scripture for your group session, a chart in the back of *When You Pray* will help you to identify which cycle to use—A, B, or C.)

Devotional Reading (5 minutes)

"Essay / Quotations"

Read aloud the brief essay written by Rueben P. Job provided for the week, as well as any quotations that you would like to share (see "Essay" and "Quotations" in *When You Pray*). Be sure to read with feeling, making the words come alive. Invite participants to close their eyes so that they may better focus on what they are hearing. If you like, invite a different group member to read aloud each week.

Journaling Time (10 minutes)
"Reflection Time"

Invite group members to write in their journals in response to the following questions:

- What is God saying to you through all that we have heard and shared today?
- How is God calling you to respond?

Encourage group members to move apart from one another as much as room setup will allow. If you like, play instrumental music quietly in the background throughout the journaling time.

(Note: For introspective groups, Journaling Time replaces Group Discussion/Application.)

Prayerwork (15-20 minutes)

Choose one of the Prayerwork ideas for introspective groups found on pages 38–40, or create/find your own prayer activity.

Group Prayer (5 minutes)
"Making Our Requests Known"

Enter into a time of prayer in which group members are invited to pray aloud in response to specific prayer prompts. Do not be afraid of silence and do not rush the process. Rather, give the Holy Spirit time to work. Pause sufficiently between the prompts so that everyone has the opportunity to pray as the Spirit leads. Use the following prompts, or feel free to create your own:

Almighty God, we offer now our praise and thanks for who you are, what you have done, and what you have revealed to us today...

Loving Creator, we now offer our prayers for our world and its people and leaders...

We lift up to you, O God, our church and its leaders...

Gracious God, receive now our prayers on behalf of those in our circle of care or concern...

Finally, Lord, we submit our personal needs and requests...

A Time of Commitment (2 minutes)
"Offering of Self to God"

Follow the group prayer with a time of commitment in which you offer your very lives to God—all that you have, all that you are, and all that you hope to become. Surrender control as you invite God to do what is best—confident that God will meet your needs and bless you as you give your life to the work of God in this world.

Invite group members to record in their journals one thing they will do in the coming week to respond to what God has shown them today. Invite them to share what they have written as they are comfortable. Then read aloud the Scripture or text provided in the weekly reading (see "Offering of Self to God" in *When You Pray*) as a prayer of commitment, or offer your own.

Closing (2 minutes)
"Blessing"

End the session with a blessing. Read aloud the blessing provided in the weekly reading (see "Blessing" in *When You Pray*), and follow it with a silent ritual that your group may repeat each week. For example, you might turn off the lights and stand silently for a moment in the light of the candle, symbolizing the presence of God that goes with you. Or you might simply leave in silence. The idea is to let the words of the blessing be the final words spoken.

Prayerwork Ideas for Introspective Groups

- Take turns sharing and discussing your own prayer practices, routines, and rituals as well as helpful hints for establishing a regular prayer habit.

- Develop a list of "Obstacles to Prayer." Have each group member create a checklist of these obstacles on a sheet of paper, leaving space for making notes in the coming week about his or her attempts to overcome these obstacles.

- Have someone present a brief teaching session on spiritual journaling. Discuss the how-to's and the benefits of keeping a prayer journal. If you like, plan a "field trip" to a nearby bookstore to purchase your own journals.

- Discuss different personality types and personal styles of prayer and spirituality. Then discover your own. Are group members extroverts or introverts? How do their personalities influence and affect their prayer practices? See Nancy Reeves' excerpt from *Spirituality for Extroverts* (Abingdon, 2008) on page 147 in *Becoming a Praying Congregation*.

- Have each group member apply a temporary tattoo as a reminder to practice daily prayer throughout the coming week. In the Middle East, Christians have century-old traditions of symbolic tattoos. In advance of the group session, research Coptic and other tattoo history and purposes and report your findings to the group; or ask a group member to conduct research in the coming week and report back next session.

- Have someone bring in a recording of music that correlates to the topic for the week. Instruct participants to meditate and/or journal while listening to the music. If you like, repeat this exercise each session, having a different participant bring in a musical recording that is somehow connected to the session's reading.

- Explore guided imagery prayer together. Research this prayer practice in advance and come prepared to lead the group through a guided imagery prayer exercise. (You can find examples on the Internet, or create your own guided prayer exercise.)

- Introduce the group to either *lectio divina* or centering prayer (or introduce one method during one session and the other method during another):

Lectio Divina

Lectio divina is a method of prayer in which you read and meditate on Scripture with the purpose of drawing closer to God as you gain insight into God's Word. Choose a Scripture passage in advance, and use this simple *lectio divina* exercise for 10-15 minutes:

- *Read* – Slowly read the passage. Approach it with reverence and expectation, savoring each word and phrase. Read a particular word or phrase that touches you, resonates with you, or even disturbs you.

- *Reflect* – Ponder this word or phrase for a few minutes. Let it sink in slowly and deeply. Ask what the word or phrase may be saying to you, or what it may be demanding of you.

- *Express* – Express to God whatever prayers may be arising within you in response to the word or phrase. They may be prayers of thanksgiving, petition, intercession, lament, or praise. If you want, you may write your prayers or thoughts.

- *Restate* – Allow yourself to sit quietly for a few moments, keeping your heart open to the fullness of God's love and peace.

Centering Prayer

Centering prayer, which places a strong emphasis on interior silence, clears the mind of rational thought in order to focus on the indwelling presence of God. Use the following simple centering prayer exercise for 5-10 minutes:

- Sit comfortably with your eyes closed. Relax and quiet yourself.

- Choose a sacred word that expresses your desire to be in God's presence and open yourself to God's divine activity within you (i.e. Jesus, Lord, God, Savior, Abba, Divine, Shalom, Spirit, etc.).

- Repeat the word silently and let it be a symbol of your desire to be in God's presence and to be open to God's divine action within you.

- Whenever you become aware of anything (thoughts, feelings, perceptions, images, associations, etc.), simply return to your sacred word.

ARTS-FOCUSED GROUP
Session Plan Template

(Note: This template outlines a session of just under 60 minutes. To decrease the time, eliminate one or more segments of your choosing. To extend the session, allow more time for Prayerwork and/or Group Discussion/Application.)

Materials Needed:
Bible(s), *When You Pray: Daily Practices for Prayerful Living*, visual element (see "Opening" below), butcher/bulletin board paper, colored pencils or markers, tape, audio Bible and CD player (optional), any items needed for your Prayerwork activity

Opening (1-3 minutes)
"Becoming Aware of God's Presence"

The opening is a time to relax and prepare yourselves for encountering God. Read aloud a brief Scripture passage intended to help group members focus their minds and hearts on recognizing and welcoming God's presence (see "Becoming Aware of God's Presence" in *When You Pray*). Display a photo, painting, sculpture, or other visual element pertaining to the Scripture or the lesson's theme for participants to focus on during this time.

Invitational Prayer (3 minutes)
"Inviting God's Intervention"

Spend a few moments inviting our Creator God to act—in your lives, your families, your small group, your church, your community, and your world. After reading aloud the brief Scripture or text provided in the weekly reading (see "Inviting God's Intervention" in *When You Pray*), offer a prayer in response. Offer praise for God's creative nature, and acknowledge the diverse gifts of creativity given to each of us. Determine in advance who will pray aloud for the group each week.

Scripture Reading (3-5 minutes)
"Listening for God's Voice"

Open yourselves to what God is saying to you through the Scriptures. Read aloud one or two key Scripture readings from those provided for the selected week (see "Listening for God's Voice" in *When You Pray*). Select the reading(s) prior to the group session. If you like, have a different group member read the Scripture selection(s) each week. If you have participants with gifts in the dramatic arts, encourage them to prepare a dramatic reading of the Scripture from week to week. Or, if you have access to an audio Bible, you might choose to play a recording of the Scripture.

(Note: In *When You Pray*, three choices are provided for the Sunday Scripture drawn from the common lectionary. If your congregation follows the Ecumenical Sunday Lectionary Scripture readings and you wish to choose a Sunday Scripture for your group session, a chart in the back of *When You Pray* will help you to identify which cycle to use—A, B, or C.)

Devotional Reading (5 minutes)
"Essay / Quotations"

Read aloud the brief essay written by Rueben P. Job provided for the selected week, as well as any quotations that you would like to share (see "Essay" and "Quotations" in *When You Pray*). If you like, invite a different group member to read aloud each week.

Group Discussion/Application (5-10 minutes)
"Reflection Time"

Take a few minutes to briefly respond to all that you have seen and heard today. In advance of the session, choose from the following questions, or feel free to write your own questions that are relevant to the theme and content of the session.

- What is God saying to you through what we have shared today?
- What thoughts and feelings does today's visual aid evoke?
- What questions have been raised by today's session?
- How is God calling you to respond—as individuals and as a group?

Prayerwork (15-20 minutes)

Choose one of the Prayerwork ideas for arts-focused groups found on pages 46–47, or create/find your own prayer activity.

Group Prayer (5 minutes)
"Making Our Requests Known"

Invite participants to create a "prayer mural" by responding creatively to specific prayer prompts (see next page). Spread out a long sheet of butcher/bulletin board paper and distribute colored pencils or markers. Encourage participants to sketch, draw, or doodle as they respond silently to each prayer prompt. Pause for one full minute after reading each prompt. Use the following prayer prompts, or feel free to create your own:

Almighty God, we offer now our praise and thanks for who you are, what you have done, and what you have revealed to us today...

Loving Creator, we now offer our prayers for our world and its people and leaders...

We lift up to you, O God, our church and its leaders...

Gracious God, receive now our prayers on behalf of those in our circle of care or concern...

Finally, Lord, we submit our personal needs and requests...

A Time of Commitment (2 minutes)
"Offering of Self to God"

Follow the group prayer with a time of commitment in which you offer your very lives to God—all that you have, all that you are, and all that you hope to become. Surrender control as you invite God to do what is best—confident that God will meet your needs and bless you as you give your life to the work of God in this world. Use the Scripture or text provided in the weekly reading (see "Offering of Self to God" in *When You Pray*) as your prayer of commitment, or offer your own prayer. After the prayer, work together to tape your prayer mural on a wall or board. Add a new prayer mural to the display each week.

Closing (2 minutes)
"Blessing"

End the session with a blessing. Call the group's attention back to the visual element used in the opening of the session. As participants focus on the visual element, read aloud the blessing provided in the weekly reading (see "Blessing" in *When You Pray*). If you like, follow the blessing with a musical benediction that the group may sing together each week. For example, you might sing a portion of "God Be With You Till We Meet Again," "Shalom to You," or some other benediction.

Prayerwork Ideas for Arts-Focused Groups

- Start a prayer project as a group. Try something tangible such as creating an altar cloth, quilt, prayer beads, or other project and work on it periodically or at each session. Pray over each part/section that you make.

- Discuss how to create "arts-focused" prayer partners or groups, such as a musical ensemble, a knitting and prayer club, and so forth.

- Have someone bring in a piece of music or art that correlates to the topic for the week. Then have participants journal, meditate, or create their own art while listening to/observing the piece. (This could be repeated each session with a different participant/leader bringing in art/music that is meaningful to him/her and somehow connected to the session reading.)

- Compile personalized "Prayer Books" or boxes of "Prayer Cards" for those who are ill or suffering in your congregation.

- Create prayer shawls or other items for people in the congregation who are going through illness, loss, or even celebration. (See the article by Andy Langford on page 114 in *Becoming a Praying Congregation*.)

- Invite a guest musician, singer, or artist to come and talk to the group about how faith influences his or her artistic expression, and vice versa.

- Create beautiful handmade cards expressing get-well, sympathy, and other uplifting messages. Send the cards to appropriate persons on your church's prayer list.

- Discuss how music, art, and other artistic expressions both evoke worship and help us to worship. How would your experience of God be different without these expressions of beauty? How would your worship be different? Brainstorm new ways you might use the arts to enrich your worship experience—both privately and corporately.

HABIT BREAKER GROUP
Session Plan Template

(Note: This template outlines a session of just under 60 minutes. To decrease the time, eliminate one or more segments of your choosing. To extend the session, allow more time for Prayerwork and/or Group Discussion/Application.)

Materials Needed:
Bibles (various translations), *When You Pray: Daily Practices for Prayerful Living*, a piece of paper or index card for each participant, pencils or pens, any items needed for your Prayerwork activity

Opening (1-3 minutes)
"Becoming Aware of God's Presence"

The opening is a time to relax and prepare yourselves for encountering God. Read aloud a brief Scripture passage intended to help group members focus their minds and hearts on recognizing and welcoming God's presence (see "Becoming Aware of God's Presence" in *When You Pray*).

Invitational Prayer (3 minutes)
"Inviting God's Intervention"

Spend a few moments inviting God to act—in your lives, your families, your small group, your church, your community, and your world. After reading aloud the brief Scripture or text provided in the weekly reading (see "Inviting God's Intervention" in *When You Pray*), offer a prayer in response. Determine in advance who will pray aloud for the group each week.

Scripture Reading (3-5 minutes)
"Listening for God's Voice"

Open yourselves to what God is saying to you through the Scriptures. Read aloud one or two key Scripture readings from those provided for the selected week (see "Listening for God's Voice" in *When You Pray*). Select the reading(s) prior to the group session. If you like, have a different group member read the Scripture selection(s) each week. Read from a different Bible translation each week to introduce new versions to participants, and/or read each Scripture from several different translations.

(Note: In *When You Pray*, three choices are provided for the Sunday Scripture drawn from the common lectionary. If your congregation follows the Ecumenical Sunday Lectionary Scripture readings and you wish to choose a Sunday Scripture for your group session, a chart in the back of *When You Pray* will help you to identify which cycle to use—A, B, or C.)

Devotional Reading (5 minutes)
"Essay / Quotations"

Read aloud the brief essay written by Rueben P. Job provided for the selected week, as well any quotations that you would like to share (see "Essay" and "Quotations" in *When You Pray*). Encourage participants to listen for insights or perspectives that might bring new understanding or fresh application to their prayer lives.

Group Discussion/Application (5-10 minutes)
"Reflection Time"

Take time to reflect on what you have read and heard and consider how it applies to your lives. In advance of the session, choose from the following questions, or feel free to write your own:

- What is God saying to you through what we have shared today?
- What new insights have you gained
- What questions have been raised by today's session?
- How is God calling you to respond—as individuals and as a group?
- What new practices would you like to try in the coming week?

Prayerwork (15-20 minutes)

Choose one of the Prayerwork ideas for habit breaker groups found on pages 54–55, or create/find your own prayer activity.

Group Prayer (5 minutes)
"Making Our Requests Known"

Enter into a time of prayer in which group members are invited to pray in response to specific prayer prompts (see next page). Try a different method of response each week. For example, one week participants might voice their prayers aloud. On other weeks they might write their prayer responses, pray silently, respond with Scripture prayers (provide participants with a list of possible Scriptures), or read aloud a responsive prayer in unison (invite a participant to write responses in advance and make copies for everyone). Be creative!

Use the following prompts, or feel free to create your own. Pause for one full minute after reading each prompt:

Almighty God, we offer now our praise and thanks for who you are, what you have done, and what you have revealed to us today...

Loving Creator, we now offer our prayers for our world and its people and leaders...

We lift up to you, O God, our church and its leaders...

Gracious God, receive now our prayers on behalf of those in our circle of care or concern...

Finally, Lord, we submit our personal needs and requests...

A Time of Commitment (2 minutes)
"Offering of Self to God"

Follow the group prayer with a time of commitment in which you offer your very lives to God—all that you have, all that you are, and all that you hope to become. Surrender control as you invite God to do what is best—confident that God will meet your needs and bless you as you give your life to the work of God in this world. Use the Scripture or text provided in the weekly reading (see "Offering of Self to God" in *When You Pray*) as your prayer of commitment, or offer your own prayer. Invite each participant to respond by writing on an index card or piece of paper a specific action he or she will take in the coming week to deepen his or her prayer life.

Closing (2 minutes)
"Blessing"

End the session with a blessing. Read aloud the blessing provided in the weekly reading (see "Blessing" in *When You Pray*), and follow it with some kind of closing that the group may participate in together. Change the closing each week. For example, one week the group might recite or sing a benediction. Another week they might offer words or gestures of love and affirmation. Invite participants to suggest creative closing ideas.

Prayerwork Ideas for
Habit Breaker Groups

- It takes about thirty days to break a habit. Likewise, it takes the same amount of time to form a new one. Make a commitment to be more intentional about prayer for the next thirty days. Talk about what this might involve. Formalize your commitment by writing a statement of commitment together. Then have everyone sign it. Talk about ways you can encourage one another and hold one another accountable. Consider choosing accountability partners as one possibility.

- Add freshness to your prayer life by praying "like children." Choose one or more simple prayers or activities to try. (Research activities and prayers online or see ideas in children's church curriculum, such as *All-in-One Bible Fun* [Abingdon, 2009].)

- Experiment with different kinds of prayer. Research prayer practices such as breath prayer, centering prayer, meditation, *lectio divina*, prayer walks or labyrinths, and so forth. Choose new styles to try each week.

- Learn about the prayer methods of other religions. Ask a different member each session to bring a topic to present and discuss. Possibilities might include Islamic calls to prayer, uses of prayer beads and rosaries, or icons. (See the article by Marilyn Thornton on page 47 and the article on prayer beads by Sally Dyck on page 156 in *Becoming a Praying Congregation*.)

- Ask participants to talk about where and how they usually pray. Then discuss new locations (perhaps outside) and new ways of prayer (e.g., kneeling if one does not usually kneel when praying). Make a list of ways to "shake up" group members' prayer practices. Pick one of the ideas and try it together.

• Brainstorm how to start a "Prayer Line" in your congregation. Talk to your pastor or church leadership about the possibility. This can be done many ways (telephone, email, website, broadcast). Read an example of how one church opened a call line during its worship service, taking calls and praying with callers, and came to have a 24/7 call line for prayer messages (see page 102 in *Becoming a Praying Congregation*).

• Learn from the example of others. Read about the spiritual lives and prayer practices of well-known saints through the centuries, both ancient and contemporary. Begin with the example of Jesus. Then ask each participant to choose an individual, research his/her habits, and report back to the group.

• Discuss creative activities that can help to facilitate prayer or serve as expressions of prayer—such as walking, moving, dancing, singing, playing an instrument, painting or drawing, or creating something. Share experiences of how creative outlets have enriched participants' prayer lives or experiences of God. Encourage everyone to choose a new activity to try in combination with prayer in the coming week.

GROUP SESSION SAMPLES

Sample Session 1
DISCUSSION-BASED GROUP

(Based on Week 23 in *When You Pray*)

Materials Needed:
Bible(s), *When You Pray: Daily Practices for Prayerful Living*

Opening (1-3 minutes)
"Becoming Aware of God's Presence"

Read aloud the following Scripture passage to help group members focus their minds and hearts on recognizing and welcoming God's presence:

My heart is steadfast, O God, my heart is steadfast;
    I will sing and make melody.
    Awake, my soul! . . .
For your steadfast love is higher than the heavens,
    and your faithfulness reaches to the clouds. *(Psalm 108:1, 4)*

Invitational Prayer (3 minutes)
"Inviting God's Intervention"

Spend a few moments inviting God to act—in your lives, your families, your small group, your church, your community, and your world. Read aloud the following Scripture:

Give justice to the weak and the orphan;
    maintain the right of the lowly and the destitute.
Rescue the weak and the needy;
    deliver them from the hand of the wicked. *(Psalm 82:3-4)*

Now have someone offer a prayer in response to the Scripture. (Determine in advance who will pray aloud for the group.)

Scripture Reading (3-5 minutes)
"Listening for God's Voice"

Open yourselves to what God is saying to you through the Scriptures. Read aloud the following:

Blessed be the LORD,
    for he has heard the sound of my pleadings.
The LORD is my strength and my shield;
    in him my heart trusts;
so I am helped, and my heart exults,
    and with my song I give thanks to him.

The LORD is the strength of his people;
    he is the saving refuge of his anointed.
O save your people, and bless your heritage;
    be their shepherd, and carry them forever. *(Psalm 28:6-9)*

Blessed be the God and Father of our Lord Jesus Christ! By his great mercy he has given us a new birth into a living hope through the resurrection of Jesus Christ from the dead, and into an inheritance that is imperishable, undefiled, and unfading, kept in heaven for you, who are being protected by the power of God through faith for a salvation ready to be revealed in the last time. In this you rejoice, even if now for a little while you have had to suffer various trials, so that the genuineness of your faith—being more precious than gold that, though perishable, is tested by fire—may be found to result in praise and glory and honor when Jesus Christ is revealed. Although you have not seen him, you love him; and even though you do not see him now, you believe in him and rejoice with an indescribable and glorious joy, for you are receiving the outcome of your faith, the salvation of your souls. *(1 Peter 1:3-9)*

Devotional Reading (5 minutes)
"Essay / Quotations"

Read aloud this brief essay written by Rueben P. Job, along with the following quotations.

Essay
Thomas wanted to see for himself. Paul when giving witness to the Church at Corinth used his own experience of the living Christ as proof of the reality of the Resurrection. We can understand the desire for that once-and-for-all physical proof that Jesus is alive and in our midst. When our dreams are cruelly crushed, as were those that Thomas had, we too begin to wonder, can we really trust Jesus and his promise to never forsake us? Or, are we on our own? Two thousand years of history tell us, "Yes, we can trust him," and, "No, we are never alone." God has granted the gift of long life to me and while I have never put my hands in the wounds of Jesus, I am more confident than ever that God is with me and that the testimony of the early church is trustworthy. "I am convinced that neither death, nor life, nor angels, nor rulers, nor things present, nor things to come, nor powers, nor height, nor depth, nor anything else in all creation, will be able to separate us from the love of God in Christ Jesus our Lord" (Romans 8:38-39). This is enough for me. How about you?

Quotations
Answers do come to prayers, both clear and unclear answers. What starts as an anxious query to God—"Are you there?

Do you hear me?"—or a defiant demand—"Prove it to me! Show me a sign!"—turns into fear in the presence of the holy. What begins as worry that our prayers are not answered, ends, if we keep praying, in awe that answers really do come. When that happens, we grow cautious about what we pray for. (*Primary Speech: A Psychology of Prayer*, Ann and Barry Ulanov [John Knox Press, 1982]; p. 99)

The story does not end there. Early in the morning two days later Mary Magdalene and the other women disciples went to the tomb with oils for a last anointing of Jesus' body. Instead of a corpse they encountered the living Christ and bore witness of this to the other disciples. As events raced on the conviction of faith rose up: The raising of the dead which was supposed to happen on the last day with the coming of the reign of God has already begun to happen. By the loving power of God Jesus is transformed into glory, he is raised up. Such existence is beyond our imagination, for it is life in another dimension beyond the limits of time and space; it is life in the dimension of God. It is better symbolized in the Easter Vigil liturgy, with its dramatic scenes of light out of darkness, proclamation of the creation story, sprinkling the water of new life, and sharing the eucharistic bread. Rather than coming to nothing in death, Jesus died into God. He is risen, whole and entire, as the embodied person he was in this life—his wounds are a sign of that. (*Consider Jesus*, Elizabeth A. Johnson [Crossroad, 1990]; pp. 59–60)

Group Discussion/Application (10 minutes)

"Reflection Time"

Take time to reflect on what you have read and heard and consider how it applies to your lives. Choose from the following questions:

- What is God saying to you about trusting God through the Scripture and other readings we have shared today?
- How does the theme of trusting God apply to a particular situation or circumstance you are dealing with currently?
- What life experiences have enlightened your understanding of what it means to trust God?
- What questions do you have related to trusting God?
- How is God calling you to respond?

Prayerwork (10 minutes)

Invite participants to define prayer. Ask: What is it? How do we do it? Why do we do it? Discuss what we can do to prevent our prayer time from becoming a "one-way conversation."

Group Prayer (5 minutes)
"Making Our Requests Known"

Enter into a time of prayer in which group members are invited to pray silently and/or aloud in response to specific prayer prompts. Use the following prompts, or feel free to create your own:

Almighty God, we offer now our praise and thanks for who you are, what you have done, and what you have revealed to us today...

Loving Creator, we now offer our prayers for our world and its people and leaders...

We lift up to you, O God, our church and its leaders...

Gracious God, receive now our prayers on behalf of those in our circle of care or concern...

Finally, Lord, we submit our personal needs and requests...

A Time of Commitment (2 minutes)

"Offering of Self to God"

In this time of commitment, offer your very lives to God—all that you have, all that you are, and all that you hope to become. Surrender control as you invite God to do what is best—confident that God will meet your needs and bless you as you give your life to the work of God in this world. Use the following Scripture as a prayer of commitment, or offer your own:

> But I trusted in your steadfast love;
> my heart shall rejoice in your salvation.
> I will sing to the LORD,
> because he has dealt bountifully with me. *(Psalm 13:5-6)*

Closing (2 minutes)

"Blessing"

Read aloud the following Scripture blessing:

> The LORD bless you and keep you;
> the LORD make his face to shine
> upon you, and be gracious to you;
> the LORD lift up his countenance upon you,
> and give you peace. *(Numbers 6:24-26)*

Follow the blessing with a benediction that the group may recite together each week. For example, you might say together, "May the Lord bless you and keep you," "Live in peace, and the God of love and peace will be with you," "The grace of our Lord Jesus Christ be with you," or some other benediction of your choosing.

Sample Session 2
INTROSPECTIVE GROUP

(Based on Week 46 in *When You Pray*)

Materials Needed:
Bible(s), *When You Pray: Daily Practices for Prayerful Living*, journals or notebooks (one for each participant), pens or pencils, candle and matches or lighter, instrumental music CD and CD player

Opening (3 minutes)
"Becoming Aware of God's Presence"

The opening is a time to relax and prepare yourselves for encountering God. Light a candle to acknowledge God's presence, and let the candle burn throughout the session. After welcoming participants, read aloud the following Scripture passage intended to help group members focus their minds and hearts on recognizing and welcoming God's presence:

> Praise the LORD!
>> Happy are those who fear the LORD,
>> who greatly delight in his commandments. *(Psalm 112:1)*

Now invite group members to sit quietly for a moment, meditating on the verse they heard as they relax and calm their bodies, minds, and spirits. You may want to play quiet instrumental music during this time.

Invitational Prayer (3 minutes)

"Inviting God's Intervention"

Spend a few moments inviting God to act—in your lives, your families, your small group, your church, your community, and your world. Read aloud the following Scripture:

Help me, O LORD my God!
  Save me according to your steadfast love.
Let them know that this is your hand;
  you, O LORD, have done it. *(Psalm 109:26-27)*

Now have someone offer a prayer in response. Determine in advance who will pray aloud for the group. (You also may choose to continue playing instrumental music during this time.)

Scripture Reading (3 minutes)

"Listening for God's Voice"

Open yourselves to what God is saying to you through the Scriptures. Read aloud the following Scripture:

Do not judge, so that you may not be judged. For with the judgment you make you will be judged, and the measure you give will be the measure you get. Why do you see the speck in your neighbor's eye, but do not notice the log in your own eye? Or how can you say to your neighbor, 'Let me take the speck out of your eye,' while the log is in your own eye? You hypocrite, first take the log out of your own eye, and then you will see clearly to take the speck out of your neighbor's eye. *(Matthew 7:1-5)*

Instruct participants to write meaningful words or phrases or make sketches in their journals as the Scripture is read.

Devotional Reading (3-5 minutes)

"Essay / Quotations"

Read aloud this brief essay written by Rueben P. Job, along with the following quotation. Be sure to read with feeling, making the words comes alive. Invite participants to close their eyes so that they may better focus on what they are hearing.

Essay

Forgiveness is a life-and-death matter because forgiveness lies at the very heart of Christian belief and practice. To remove forgiveness from our theology and practice is to tear the heart out of any hope of faithful Christian discipleship, and it is to drive a stake through the heart of Christian community.

This is the reality we confess every time we pray as Jesus taught us to pray. Forgiveness can never be taken lightly by those who consider their own need of forgiveness. The words of Jesus that we pray bind our need for forgiveness firmly to our willingness to forgive. Forgiveness is not only a preposterous gift; it is unbelievably difficult and costly. That is why we may talk about it easily and practice it with such difficulty. To offer forgiveness to a national enemy today will most likely be branded as unpatriotic and to extend forgiveness to another is often branded as being soft and unrealistic. But the forgiveness Jesus taught and practiced is neither soft nor unpatriotic. But it is extremely costly and laden with a mother load of grace for those who practice it. To follow Jesus and adopt his value as our own is to love our enemies and desire their good even when they inflict pain and suffering on those we love. The words of Jesus from the cross, "Father forgive them; for they do not know what they are doing," become the final demonstration on how to forgive. His words and action make me realize anew the unparalleled importance of forgiveness and my own timid practice that should be a way of life.

Quotation

When Jesus taught his disciples to pray, he grabbed hold of vertical forgiveness, "O Lord, forgive me, for I have sinned," and nailed it to horizontal forgiveness, "...as we forgive those who trespass against us," two interrelated acts of forgiveness, forming a cross. Jesus not only taught about forgiveness. He became forgiveness. He makes forgiveness possible and real. (*The Beautiful Work of Learning to Pray*, James C. Howell [Abingdon, 2003]; p. 73)

Journaling Time (10 minutes)

"Reflection Time"

Invite group members to write in their journals in response to the following questions:

- What is God saying to you through all that we have heard and shared today?
- How is God calling you to respond?

Encourage group members to move apart from one another as much as room setup will allow. If you like, play instrumental music quietly in the background throughout the journaling time.

Prayerwork (10-20 minutes)

Have someone present a brief teaching session on spiritual journaling. Discuss the how-to's and the benefits of keeping a prayer journal. If you like, plan a "field trip" to a nearby bookstore to purchase your own journals.

Group Prayer (5-7 minutes)
"Making Our Requests Known"

Enter into a time of prayer in which group members are invited to pray aloud in response to specific prayer prompts. Do not be afraid of silence and do not rush the process. Rather, give the Holy Spirit time to work. Pause sufficiently between the prompts so that everyone has the opportunity to pray as the Spirit leads. Use the following prompts, or feel free to create your own:

Almighty God, we offer now our praise and thanks for who you are, what you have done, and what you have revealed to us today...

Loving Creator, we now offer our prayers for our world and its people and leaders...

We lift up to you, O God, our church and its leaders...

Gracious God, receive now our prayers on behalf of those in our circle of care or concern...

Finally, Lord, we submit our personal needs and requests...

A Time of Commitment (2 minutes)

"Offering of Self to God"

Follow the group prayer with a time of commitment in which you offer your very lives to God—all that you have, all that you are, and all that you hope to become. Surrender control as you invite God to do what is best—confident that God will meet your needs and bless you as you give your life to the work of God in this world.

Invite group members to take turns sharing aloud one thing they will do in the coming week to respond to what God has shown them today. (Have them record this in their journals.) Then read aloud the following Scripture:

Praise the LORD!
I will give thanks to the LORD with my whole heart,
   in the company of the upright, in the congregation.

(Psalm 111:1)

Closing (2 minutes)

"Blessing"

Read aloud the following blessing:

For you shall go out in joy,
   and be led back in peace;
the mountains and the hills before you
   shall burst into song,
   and all the trees of the field shall clap their hands.

(Isaiah 55:12)

End with a silent ritual that your group may repeat each week. For example, you might turn off the lights and stand silently for a moment in the light of the candle, symbolizing the presence of God that goes with you. Or you might simply leave in silence. The idea is to let the words of the blessing be the final words spoken.